ROSALYN SCHANZER

HarperCollinsPublishers

The artwork in this book was done with colored dyes and sepia pen line on Strathmore bristol board. Blotter paper was used on the damp dye to attain a textured effect. The initial caps in this book reflect Benjamin Franklin's work as a printer. They are set in Caslon Antique, a version of the typeface he brought to America in the 1740s.

I would like to extend a special thanks to Roy E. Goodman, assistant librarian and curator of printed materials at the American Philosophical Society Library in Philadelphia, for reviewing this manuscript and for generously directing me to many rare materials and publications to use for research. If there are any errors in the book, they are solely my own.

The images on the endpapers are courtesy of the American Philosophical Society. A few of the books I used for both editorial and pictorial content include *The Papers of Benjamin Franklin*, Yale University Press; *The Autobiography of Benjamin Franklin* by Benjamin Franklin; *Poor Richard's Almanack* by Benjamin Franklin; *The Ingenious Dr. Franklin* by Nathan G. Goodman; *The First American: The Life and Times of Benjamin Franklin* by H. W. Brands; *Benjamin Franklin, Scientist and Statesman* by I. Bernard Cohen; 1975 *Antiques* magazine article "Mr. Cram's Fan Chair" by Charles B. Wood; *Due Reverence* by Murphy D. Smith; *Antiques in the Possession of the American Philosophical Society* by Murphy D. Smith; *Benjamin Franklin's "Good House"* (National Park Service pamphlet) by Claude-Anne Lopez.

—✕❊ To Fig ❊✕—

How Ben Franklin Stole the Lightning
Copyright © 2003 by Rosalyn Schanzer   Manufactured in China.
All rights reserved.   www.harperchildrens.com
Library of Congress Cataloging-in-Publication Data   Schanzer, Rosalyn.
How Ben Franklin stole the lightning / Rosalyn Schanzer.   p.   cm.
Summary: Focuses on Benjamin Franklin's role as an inventor of whimsical gadgets and practical contraptions, with an emphasis on his experiment of flying a kite during a rainstorm.
ISBN 0-688-16993-7 — ISBN 0-688-16994-5 (lib. bdg.)
1. Franklin, Benjamin, 1706–1790—Knowledge—Physics—Juvenile literature.
2. Electricity—Experiments—History—Juvenile literature.   3. Lightning—Experiments—History—Juvenile literature.   4. Physicists—United States—Biography—Juvenile literature.
[1. Franklin, Benjamin, 1706–1790.   2. Scientists.   3. Lightning—Experiments—History.]
I. Title.   QC16.F58 S33   2003   530'.092—dc21   [B]   2001039498
Typography by Carla Weise
1   2   3   4   5   6   7   8   9   10
❖
First Edition

"We are, I think, in the right
Road of Improvement, for
we are making Experiments."

—Benjamin Franklin

It's true!

The great Benjamin Franklin really did steal lightning right out of the sky! And then he set out to tame the beast. It goes to figure, though, because he was a man who could do just about anything.

Why, Ben Franklin could swim faster, argue better, and write funnier stories than practically anyone in colonial America. He was a musician, a printer, a cartoonist, and a world traveler! What's more, he was a newspaper owner, a shopkeeper, a soldier, and a politician. He even helped to write the Declaration of Independence *and* the Constitution of the United States!

en was always coming up with newfangled ways to help folks out, too. He was the guy who started the first lending library in America. His post office was the first to deliver mail straight to people's houses.

He also wrote almanacs that gave hilarious advice about life and told people when to plant crops, whether there might be an eclipse, and when the tides would be high or low.

And he helped to start a hospital!

A free academy!

A fire department!

In colonial days, fire could break out at any time. And it was lightning that caused some of the worst fires. Many people believed that being struck by lightning was a punishment from God. Whenever thunderstorms were brewing, they would ring the church bells for all they were worth, but it didn't do anybody a lick of good.

Of course, after Ben stole the lightning, there weren't nearly as many fires for firefighters to put out. "Now, why was that?" I hear you ask. "And how did he steal any lightning in the first place?" Well, it's a long story, but before we get to the answer, here's a hint. One of the things Benjamin Franklin liked to do best was to make inventions.

Why, Ben was a born inventor. He loved to swim fast, but he wanted to go even faster. So one day when he was a mere lad of eleven, he got some wood and invented swim paddles for his hands and swim fins for his feet. Ben could go faster, all right, but the wood was pretty heavy, and his wrists got plum worn out.

That's why his second invention was a better way to go fast. He lay on his back, held on to a kite string, and let his kite pull him lickety-split across a big pond. (You might want to remember later on that Ben always did like kites.)

Ben kept right on inventing better ways to do things for the rest of his life.

Take books, for example. Ben read so many books that some of them sat on shelves way up high near the ceiling. So he invented the library chair. If he pulled up the seat, out popped some stairs to help him reach any books on high shelves. And in case climbing stairs made him dizzy, he invented a long wooden arm that could grab his books, too.

He also invented an odometer that told how far he had ridden to deliver the mail. And the first clock with a second hand. And he even thought up daylight saving time. Then he invented bifocals so older folks could see up close and far away without changing glasses.

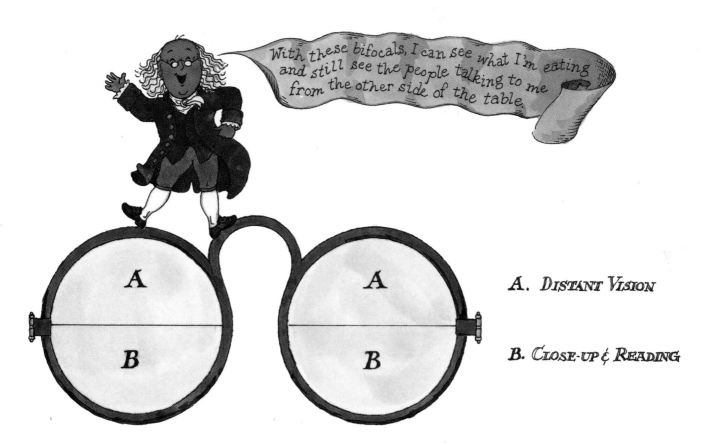

With these bifocals, I can see what I'm eating and still see the people talking to me from the other side of the table.

A. DISTANT VISION

B. CLOSE-UP & READING

Everybody and his brother and sister just had to find better ways to heat their houses in wintertime. So Ben came up with a Franklin stove that could warm up cold rooms faster and use a lot less wood than old-fashioned stoves and fireplaces.

People all over Europe and America loved Ben's glass armonica. This instrument could spin wet glass bowls to make music that sounded like it came straight from heaven. Mozart and Beethoven wrote music for it, and it was even played at a royal Italian wedding.

But as popular as warmer stoves and glass armonicas were, they aren't anywhere near as celebrated nowadays as the invention Ben made after he stole the lightning.

Another hint about Ben's most famous invention is that it helped make life easier for everyone. His scientific ideas were helpful, too, and were often way ahead of their time. For example, he had a lot of ideas about health. He said that exercise and weight lifting help keep folks fit, but they have to work hard enough to sweat if they want to do any good.

He wrote that breathing fresh air and drinking lots of water are good for you. He was the guy who said "an apple a day keeps the doctor away."

And before anyone ever heard of vitamin C, he wrote that oranges, limes, and grapefruit give people healthy gums and skin. Sailors soon got wind of this idea. They began eating so many limes to stop getting sick from scurvy at sea that they became known as limeys.

Didn't the man ever stop to rest? Even when he was outside, Ben kept right on experimenting.

For instance, he often sailed to England and France to do business for America. As he crossed the Atlantic Ocean, he charted the Gulf Stream by taking its temperature. Once sailors knew the route of this fast, warm "river" in the cold ocean, they could travel between America and Europe in a shorter time than ever before.

He was probably the first person to write weather forecasts, too. Once he chased a roaring whirlwind by riding over the hills and forests of Maryland just to find out how it worked.

Ben had an old scientific trick that he liked to show people every chance he got. He used to store some oil inside a bamboo walking stick, and whenever he poured a few drops onto angry waves in a pond or lake, the water became smooth as glass!

eanwhile, over in Europe, people called "electricians" had started doing some tricks of their own. One trick was to raise a boy up near the ceiling with a bunch of silk cords, rub his feet with a glass "electric tube," and make sparks shoot out of his hands and face.

Another mean trick made the king of France laugh so hard he could hardly stop. His court electrician had run an electric charge through 180 soldiers of the guard, and they jerked to attention faster than they ever had in their entire lives.

But although people were doing lots of tricks with electricity, nobody had a clue about why or how it worked. So Benjamin Franklin decided to find out. He asked a British friend to send him an electric tube so that he could do some experiments.

In one experiment, he made a cork "electric spider" with thread for legs. It kept leaping back and forth between a wire and an electric tube just like it was alive.

Another time, he asked a lady and gentleman to stand on some wax. One held an electric tube, the other held a wire, and when they tried to kiss, they got shocked by all the sparks shooting between their lips.

Ben even figured out how to light up a picture of a king in a golden frame. Anyone trying to remove the king's gold paper crown was in for a shock!

Doing all these tricks gave Ben his idea for stealing lightning out of the sky. You see, Ben did not agree that being struck by lightning was a punishment for evil deeds. He believed that lightning was nothing more nor less than pure electricity. Now he set out to prove it.

First he made a silk kite with a wire on top to attract some lightning. Next he added a kite string, tied a key to the bottom, and knotted a silk ribbon below the key. Ben and his son William stood out of the rain inside the doorway of a shed on the side of a field. To keep from getting shocked, Ben held on to the dry silk ribbon. Then he flew his kite straight up toward a big rain cloud.

For the longest time, nothing happened.

Just as Ben and William were about to give up, the hair on that wet kite string began to rise up and stand at attention. Ben put his knuckle near the key, and *YIKES!!!!* Out jumped a bright spark of genuine electricity!

Real lightning had traveled all the way down that kite string!

Ben had stolen electric fire out of the heavens and proven that he was right.

(Of course, now we know that if the storm had been any stronger, the great inventor would have been toast.)

Finally! Here's the part of the story where Ben's practice from thinking up all those inventions came in so handy. Way back then, you remember, lightning was always setting fire to ships, houses, and church spires. Even the best fire departments couldn't keep entire towns from going up in smoke. So Ben decided to make his most famous invention of all—the lightning rod!

The whole idea was to pull lightning safely out of the sky before it could do any mischief. Ben showed people how to put a pointed iron rod on the tip-top of a roof or ship's mast and connect it to a wire leading all the way down under the ground or into water. Now the lightning could follow a safe path without burning up a thing.

This simple but brilliant invention worked beautifully. It saved more lives than anyone can count and made Ben Franklin a great hero.

Scientists from around the world lined up to give Ben medals and awards. But during his long life, he became much more than the master of lightning. Why, when America fought against Great Britain for the right to become a free nation, Ben convinced France to come help win the war, and when it was over, he helped convince Great Britain to sign the peace. He had helped in so many ways that the people of France honored him with a beautiful medallion. It says "He snatched the lightning from heaven and the scepter from tyrants."

And he did.

A Note from the Author

Benjamin Franklin's famous lightning rod even saved the lives of his own family. One time when Ben was away, his neighbors heard the crack of an enormous lightning bolt hitting his house. They ran to put out the fire—but there wasn't one! His family was perfectly safe. Years later when Ben was having some work done on his roof, he discovered that the nine-inch copper point on his lightning rod had melted almost entirely away.

In the two hundred fifty years since Franklin invented the lightning rod, new uses for electric power have forever changed the way people live. Ben started things off by dreaming up some less well-known electric inventions, too. For example, he invented a simple electric motor, a battery that stored electricity, and electric bells that rang inside his house whenever lightning was in the air (this scared his wife silly).

On the endpapers in this book, you will find parts of Franklin's original drawings showing ideas for electrical experiments, sea anchors that won't snap in storms, sails designed to make ships go faster, and even a complicated "magic circle" with rows of numbers going every which way that all add up to the same total amount.

Sometimes Ben improved upon other people's inventions. For instance, he used ancient Chinese ideas to heat his bathroom and bathtub, and he probably had the first flush toilet in America. But he often gets credit for inventions he may never have made in the first place. Take the fan chair, for example. Some folks claim that Ben invented this rocking chair with a fan on top to blow away flies. Well, Ben really did own such a chair, but it was probably invented by a musical instrument maker named Mr. Cram. Then there's the Philadelphia busybody, a popular device that used three mirrors to let homeowners see who was knocking at their front doors without going downstairs. Though it is often listed as one of his inventions, the great man never once mentions it in his papers, and he wrote a lot of papers about most everything he ever did.

Here's a list of some of Ben's scientific work:

* studied mastodon fossils

* studied fish and seashell fossils and said the sea once covered areas that are mountains today

* described sea life in detail during his ocean voyages

* studied population growth

* promoted good uses of insects such as bees, silkworms, the cochineal (red dye), and Spanish flies (medicine)

* studied why supposedly dead insects sometimes come back to life

* investigated effects of the environment on birds

* fought pollution by writing that slaughterhouses, tanyards, and lime pits on the docks and nearby streets were ruining the environment

* diagrammed a waterspout

* studied eclipses and the aurora borealis

* studied the earth's magnetic poles

* said coal was ancient vegetable matter

* worked to figure out the distance from Earth to the sun

* wrote about lead poisoning (the type in Ben's printing presses was made of lead)

* wrote about gout (gout from lead gave Ben a very sore big toe)

* introduced the soybean and wrote about tofu

* made up a phonetic alphabet

* predicted that hot air balloons would be used for spying and dropping bombs during wars

Benjamin Franklin did more great things than you can shake a stick at. He helped to make Philadelphia a first-rate city, he got rich writing *Poor Richard's Almanack*, and he was a well-traveled man of the world. When he was old enough to be the father of all the other founding fathers, he convinced the French to give America desperately needed money, soldiers, and weapons for fighting the Revolutionary War. After America triumphed over British tyranny, Ben helped to write the Treaty of Paris, which granted America independence and land that extended all the way to the Mississsippi River.

So why did I decide to limit this book to Franklin's life as a scientist and inventor? It seems to me that his work in these areas shows all the best sides of this great man. He was so generous that he never patented his inventions because he wanted everyone to be able to use them for free. He was so practical that he used many of his ideas to make life safer and easier. He was so brilliant and curious about the world around him that he studied mathematics, medicine, music, weather, geology, astronomy, entomology, ecology, oceanography, and much more. He was such a hard worker that he even made studies and inventions while he was traveling to do diplomatic work for America. And his mischievous sense of humor shone through in his electrical experiments and in all of his scientific writing.

Why was Ben the most famous American in the world during his day? He once wrote, "If you would not be forgotten, as soon as you are dead and rotten, either write things worth reading or do things worth the writing." He spent a lifetime doing both.

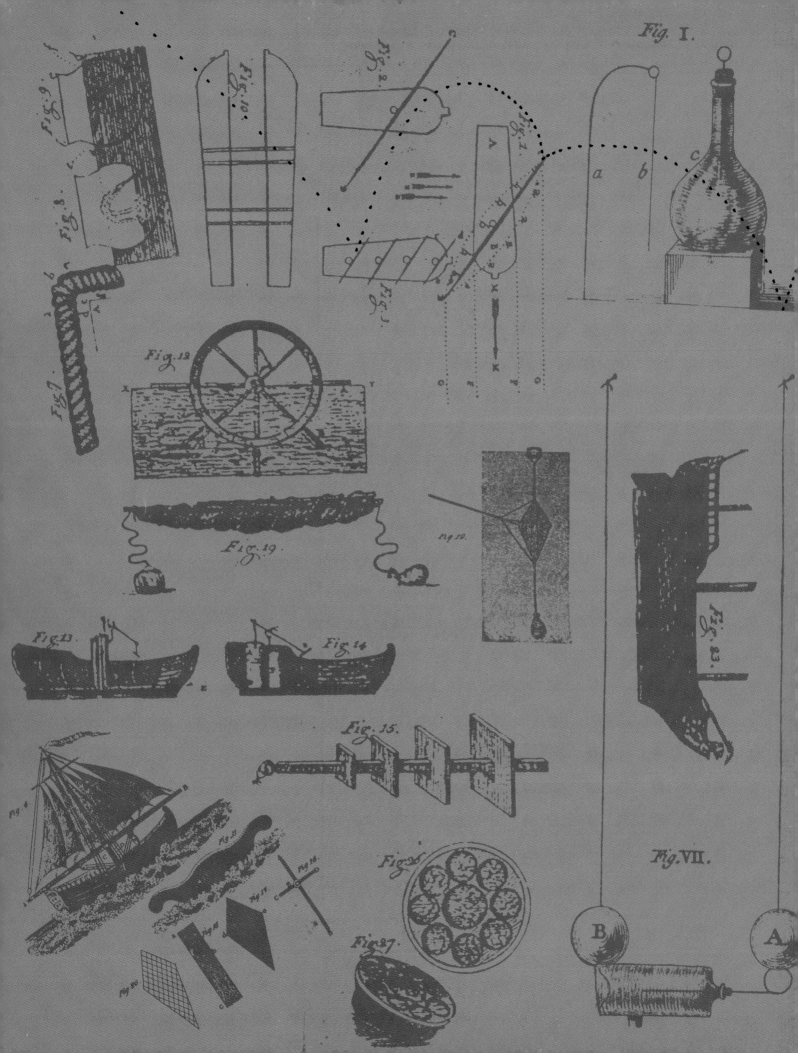

Fig. 9.

Fig. 8.

Fig. 10.

Fig. 2.

Fig. 1.

Fig. I.

a   b   c

Fig. 7.

Fig. 3.

Fig. 12.

Fig. 16.

Fig. 19.

Fig. 23.

Fig. 13.

Fig. 14.

Fig. 15.

Fig. VII.

Fig. 26.

Fig. 27.

B   A